Animal Parts

Animal Tails

By Connor Stratton

www.littlebluehousebooks.com

Little Blue House is distributed by North Star Editions:
sales@northstareditions.com | 888-417-0195

Produced for Little Blue House by Red Line Editorial.

Photographs ©: iStockphoto, cover, 4, 9 (bottom), 11 (top), 12, 17 (top), 18, 20–21, 22–23, 24 (top left), 24 (bottom left), 24 (bottom right); Shutterstock Images, 7 (top), 7 (bottom), 9 (top), 11 (bottom), 15 (top), 15 (bottom), 17 (bottom), 24 (top right)

Library of Congress Control Number: 2020900817

ISBN
978-1-64619-180-2 (hardcover)
978-1-64619-214-4 (paperback)
978-1-64619-282-3 (ebook pdf)
978-1-64619-248-9 (hosted ebook)

Printed in the United States of America
Mankato, MN
082020

About the Author

Connor Stratton enjoys spotting new animals and writing books for children. He lives in Minnesota.

Table of Contents

Kinds of Tails

Many animals have tails. Animals have tails on their back ends.

Some tails are large.

Other tails are small.

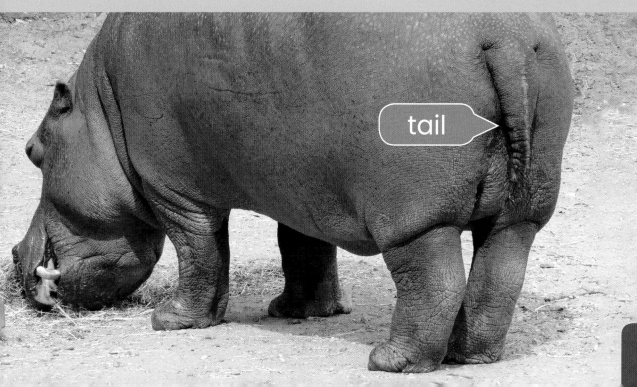

Some tails hang down.

Other tails stand up.

9

Some tails are one color.

Other tails have
many colors.

Many Animals

Many kinds of animals can have tails.

Lizards can have tails.

Fish can have tails too.

Birds can have tails.

Insects can have tails too.

17

Long Tails

Many animals have long tails.
Giraffes have the longest tails on land.

Birds can have long tails.

Their tails are feathers.

21

Lizards can have
long tails.
Their tails can be longer
than their bodies.

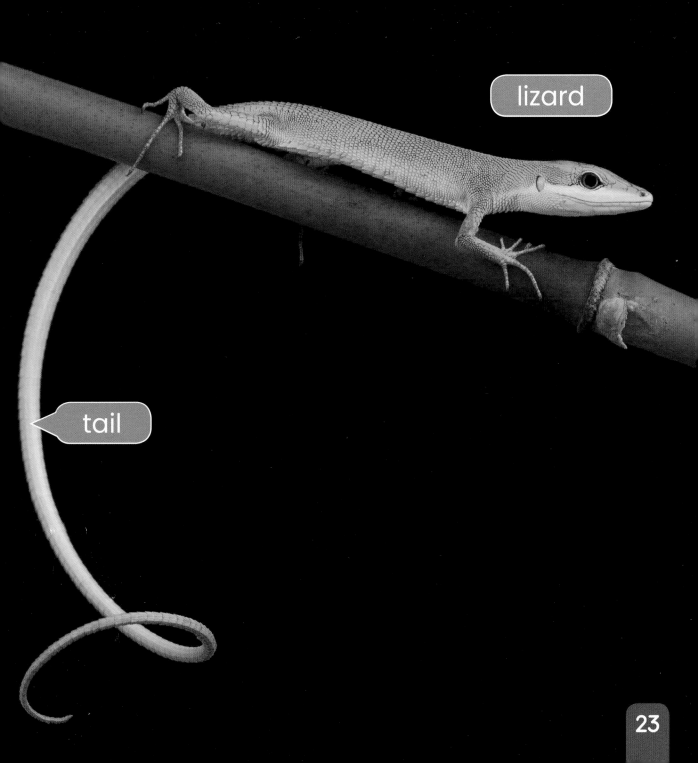

lizard

tail

Glossary

bird

insect

giraffe

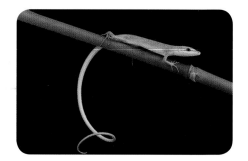

lizard

Index